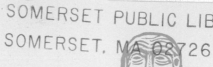

THE NORMANS

Peter Chrisp

Wayland

Look into the Past

The Ancient Chinese
The Anglo-Saxons
The Aztecs
The Egyptians
The Greeks
The Incas
The Japanese
The Maya
The Normans
The Romans
The Sioux
The Tudors & Stuarts
The Victorians
The Vikings

Series editor: Joanna Bentley
Series designer: David West
Book designer: Joyce Chester

First published in 1994 by Wayland (Publishers) Limited,
61 Western Road, Hove, East Sussex, BN3 1JD, England

British Library Cataloguing in Publication Data
    Chrisp, Peter
    Normans.–(Look into the Past series)
    I. Title II. Series
    942.021

ISBN 0 7502 1064 8

Typeset by Dorchester Typesetting Group Ltd., Dorset,
England.
Printed and bound in Italy by L.E.G.O. S.p.A., Vicenza,
Italy.

Picture acknowledgements
The publishers wish to thank the following for providing the
photographs in this book: British Museum 19; C M Dixon 22
(bottom), 24 (bottom), 27, 28, 29; E T Archive 7, 18 (top),
21, 23; Werner Forman Archive 5; Michael Holford 6, 8, 9,
10, 11, 12, 13, 14, 15, 17, 19 (top and middle), 20, 24 (top);
Topham 16, 22 (top), 25.
Map artwork by Jenny Hughes.
Artwork on page 18 by Stephen Wheele.

CONTENTS

Words that appear in **bold italic** in the text are explained in the glossary on page 30.

WHO WERE THE NORMANS?

The Normans were a warlike people from Normandy, a small area on the north coast of France. They are famous today for the conquests they made between 1030 and 1150, which are all shown on the map below. The best known conquest was that of England in 1066. But Norman knights also conquered southern Italy, Sicily, Malta, Antioch in the *Middle East* and part of north Africa. They also tried, but failed, to conquer Greece. In the 1170s a French poet called Jordan Fantosme summed up the Normans in these words: "The Normans are good conquerors. There is no race like them."

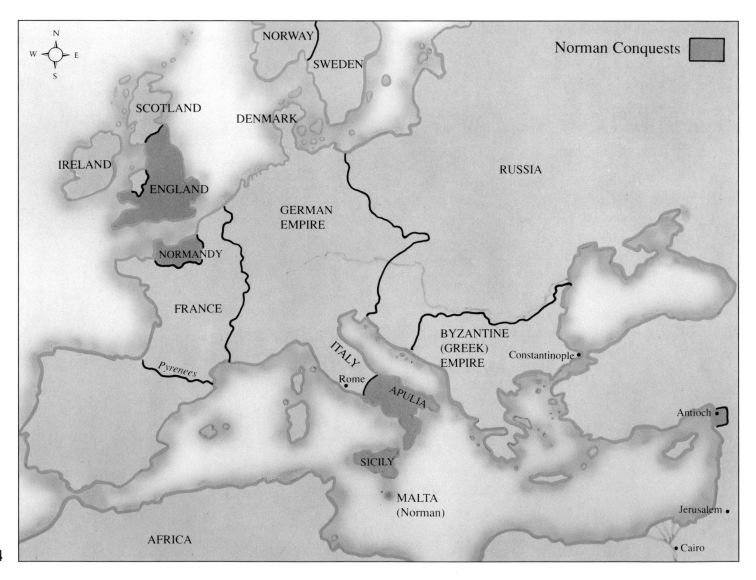

In the beginning, the Normans were *Vikings*. The word Norman means 'north man', or Viking. The Vikings were fierce raiders from Norway, Sweden and Denmark, who attacked the coasts of western Europe in their longships. You can see a Viking longship on this carved stone from Sweden. ▶

In the year 911, the French king, Charles the Simple, allowed a Viking raider called Rolf (or Rollo) to settle on the north coast of France. Charles' plan was that Rolf would defend the coast against other Vikings. The arrangement was a big success.

Rolf and his fellow Vikings gave up their old religion and became Christians. They married French women and settled down.

Within a hundred years, the Viking settlers were speaking French. The part of France they settled came to be called 'Normandy', the land of the north men. The Vikings had turned into Normans.

KNIGHTS AND HORSES

The Normans were able to win many battles thanks to their skill at fighting on horseback. From the age of seven or eight, the sons of Norman nobles learned to ride and fight. Their war horses, called destriers, were bred to be fast and strong and trained not to panic in battle. A good war horse was very expensive.

◀ Here you can see Norman knights charging into battle on their war horses. They wear small helmets with nose guards and heavy suits of chain mail (armour made from hundreds of tiny metal rings). They carry long, kite-shaped shields and light lances, used for jabbing or throwing.

◀ These two knights are using a heavier type of lance. It was gripped tightly under the arm and used like a battering ram, to knock the enemy over. These pictures come from the Bayeux Tapestry, a 70-metre-long embroidery showing the Norman conquest of England in 1066.

This Norman knight riding a stocky horse is a chess piece, from southern Italy – another place conquered by the Normans. He carries a long slashing sword, used when the lance had been broken or thrown. Chess, a game about war, was very popular with the Normans.

THE DUKE AND HIS PEOPLE

The most powerful man in Normandy was the duke. All the land belonged to him. He gave large areas to the most important nobles, who were called *barons*. They were said to 'hold' the land rather than own it. In return, the barons had to give the duke services, such as providing him with knights. They swore a solemn oath to be loyal to the duke, who was their 'overlord'.

◄This is Duke William, the great-great-great-grandson of Rolf the Viking. He ruled over Normandy from 1035 to 1087.

The barons shared out much of their land to knights in exchange for their services. These knights ruled over the villages as overlords. Other knights had no lands but gave their services for money. They lived with the baron or the duke in his *castle*. As well as fighting for their overlord, the knights had to pay for their horses and equipment and bring foot soldiers to add to the army.

In the villages, each knight allowed ordinary people to hold land. The knight also gave them his protection. In return, they provided him with services, such as working on his fields. In times of war, the men served as foot soldiers and *archers*. This system, in which everyone served an overlord, is called 'feudalism'.

9

1066: THE CONQUEST OF ENGLAND

In the 1060s England was ruled by an old king called Edward the Confessor. Edward had no sons of his own to be king after him. William of Normandy, who was distantly related to Edward, felt that he had a strong claim to the throne. Another possible king was Harold Godwinson, the most powerful nobleman in England. These pictures, from the Bayeux Tapestry, show the struggle between Harold and William for the crown of England.

◀ At first Harold and William were friends. In 1064 or 65, Harold sailed to Normandy and stayed with William. According to Norman writers, he swore to help William become king. Here Harold is swearing his oath in front of William.

◀ In 1066 King Edward of England died. Here you can see the English nobles, on the left, offering the crown to Harold. Harold accepted. He sits on the throne on the right, wearing his new crown. How do you think William felt when he heard the news?

William was furious. He quickly made plans to invade England and seize the throne. Here you can see carpenters cutting wood and building ships for the invasion fleet. ▶

The ships are loaded with weapons, heavy suits of chain mail and barrels of wine. ▼

Now the fleet, packed with horses and knights, sails for England. William's ship has a lantern on top of the mast. This was lit to keep the fleet together – the crossing took place at night, on 27 September 1066. ▼

While the Normans were crossing the sea, Harold was busy in the north of England. He was fighting another invading army, from Norway. Harold won that battle and then raced south to fight William. Their armies met near Hastings, on 14 October 1066. In these scenes, the Norman knights are fighting on horseback, while the English fight on foot. They stand in a tight row, called a 'shield wall', armed with battle axes and spears. ▶

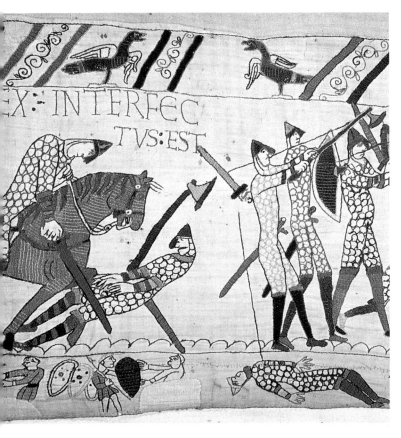

◀ The fighting lasted for eight hours. In this section, you can see how it ended. The writing says, 'Here King Harold was killed'. He may be the figure pulling an arrow from his eye, or he may be the man falling beneath the horse. Perhaps both figures show Harold at different stages of his last desperate fight.

With their king dead, the English army broke up and fled. In the lower border of the tapestry, the dead and dying English are being stripped of their armour. William had earned a new nickname, 'the Conqueror'.

CASTLES

Although the Normans had beaten the English in battle, they did not feel safe. They knew that the English hated them and might attack at any time. Between 1067 and 1071, William's army had to fight to put down several uprisings by the English nobles. To protect themselves, and to make it easier to rule their new lands, the Normans built castles. Before 1066, these were almost unknown in England. Soon there were hundreds of them. 'They filled the whole land with these castles,' wrote an English monk in the 1130s, 'and when these castles were built, they filled them with devils and wicked men.'

Here is a famous Norman castle. It is called Falaise Castle, and is the place where William the Conqueror was born.

Early Norman ▶ castles were made from wood, which could easily catch fire. This picture shows the Normans attacking the castle of Dinan in Brittany. Can you see the two Norman knights holding flaming torches up to the wooden walls? The Duke of Brittany is forced to surrender. You can see him handing the castle keys over on the end of a lance.

◀ In time the Normans replaced their wooden castles with stronger ones, made of stone. Stonemasons from Normandy did the skilled work, while most of the labouring was done by English people. This is Rochester Castle in Kent, built around 1130. The tall building in the centre is called a 'keep'. It is 40 metres high and its walls are 3.6 metres thick.

HUNTING AND FEASTING

When they were not fighting, Norman nobles loved to hunt wild animals. In those days the forests of England were full of deer and boar (wild pigs). The Normans chased them on horseback with packs of dogs. Then they killed them with their spears or with bows and arrows. This was a useful way of keeping both men and horses well trained for warfare. It was also a way of getting food, for the animals were cooked and eaten at great feasts after the day's hunting. Only the nobles were allowed to hunt these animals. If ordinary people were caught hunting, they could be killed.

▼ Here you can see some nobles hunting with their dogs and a trained hawk. This is Harold with his friends before the conquest of England. You can tell they are English because they have moustaches and their hair is longer than the Normans. English nobles liked to hunt as much as the Normans, but few of them got the chance after 1066. Most of those who were not killed in battle fled abroad.

This scene shows a feast being prepared. On ▶ the left, meat is being boiled in a pot. The man in the middle is picking up hot bread or cakes using tongs. You can also see joints of meat which have been roasted on spits, like kebabs.

Text within the tapestry image: hIC:COQVITVR:CARO ET hIC: MINISTRAVERVN MINISTRI

▼ Can you see the man blowing a horn? He is letting everyone know that the feast is ready. On the right, William and his barons are eating with knives and with their fingers – forks had not been invented. Bishop Odo, William's half-brother, is blessing the meal.

Text within the tapestry image: hIC FECERVN:PRANDIVM: ET hIC EPISCOPVS:CIBV:ET: POTV:BE NE DIC IT

17

LIFE ON THE LAND

Knights and barons made up only a tiny part of the population. Most people in Norman times worked on the land, farming. It was thanks to their work that the nobles could spend their time hunting and fighting.

The farming people belonged to different classes, depending on how much land they held. For example, villeins were farmers who had more than twelve hectares of land. Cottars had less than two hectares. At the bottom there were serfs, or slaves. They had no land at all and were treated as their lord's property.

We know about different classes of people ▶ because of the **Domesday Book**. This is a great survey of the land ordered by William in 1086. He wanted to find out everything he could about England. In particular, he wanted to know how rich his kingdom was. The Domesday Book tells us the names of people who held land throughout the kingdom. It also records the amount of land they held and what they paid in tax to the king. Even their farm animals were counted.

◀ Each village was surrounded by three huge fields, divided into strips. Every year, two of the fields were planted with wheat, oats or barley, while the third field was left *fallow*. People had strips spread out among the three fields.

The borders of the Bayeux Tapestry show us the farm work of ordinary people. Here you can see the different stages in planting crops.

On the left, a donkey is being used to pull a plough. On the right, a man is sowing seed by scattering it over the ploughed field. ▼

Now the seed is covered over using a harrow (a spiked frame) pulled by a horse. ▶

◀ This picture comes from an English calendar, painted thirty years before the Norman Conquest. It shows the work that follows the harvest (gathering) of a crop like wheat or barley. The crop is being beaten with sticks to separate the grains from the chaff (the unwanted stalks and husks). It is then tossed in the air. The chaff blows away while the heavier grains fall to the ground. It was hard work being a farmer.

19

RELIGION

The Normans were Christians, people who worship Jesus Christ. As Christians, they believed that after death everyone was judged by Christ. People who had been good Christians were rewarded in Heaven. Everyone else went down to hell, where they suffered terrible agonies for ever and ever.

▲ The teachings of Christianity are in a book called the Bible. However, in Norman times, few people could read. In any case, the Bible used in churches was written in Latin, a language that most people did not know. So people learned about Christianity from paintings, which covered the walls of every church. This painting, from Chaldon in Surrey, shows the wicked tumbling down to hell where they are tortured by devils. Meanwhile, good people, helped by angels, climb a ladder up into Heaven.

▲ When people went to worship in the
Norman *cathedral* of Monreale in Sicily, they
could see a huge figure of Jesus Christ above
their heads. His head and shoulders alone are
20 metres high. This is a mosaic, a picture
made from thousands of tiny coloured tiles.
The Normans could never forget that Jesus
was watching them and judging them.

The **Church** ►
taught that there were various ways that people could avoid going to hell. To start with, they had to be baptized – blessed with holy water from a font, or basin.

This Norman font, from Winchester, shows Saint Nicholas helping a poor man and his three daughters. Saints were people who had led holy lives and who Christians prayed to for help.

Knights believed they had their own way of getting to Heaven: going on a *crusade*. A crusade was a holy war fought against people of other religions, especially *Muslims*. The most successful was the First Crusade (1096-9), which ended in the capture of Jerusalem. Among its leaders were two famous Normans, Robert Curthose, son of William the Conqueror, and Bohemond 'the Giant', a leader of the Normans in Italy. Bohemond made himself ruler of Antioch (see page 4).

Jerusalem, the city where Christ died and was buried, was the holiest place on earth to Christians. This is a map of the world, watched over by Christ. You can see Jerusalem in the middle. Christians believed that Jerusalem lay right at the centre of the world. ▼

◄ Another way of serving Christ, and avoiding hell, was to become a *monk* or a *nun*. These were men and women who lived apart from ordinary people in monasteries and nunneries. They spent their days in prayer. This is the store house of Fountains Abbey, a monastery in Yorkshire. The king and his nobles paid for the building of monasteries. This was their way of serving Christ. They also hoped that the prayers of the monks and nuns would help them get to Heaven.

In Norman times, men who had joined the ▶ Church as priests or monks were easy to recognize – they shaved the tops of their heads. This man's rich robes are a sign that he is not just an ordinary priest. He is a *bishop*, one of the important leaders of the Church. Norman bishops were also barons – they had their own castles, and knights who fought for them.

The church where a bishop had his headquarters was called a cathedral. This was because the bishop had his 'cathedra', or seat, there. Cathedrals were the biggest structures that the Normans built. They spent huge sums of money on them, to show their love of God.

◀ This is Durham Cathedral, which towers over the city. It would have been even more impressive in Norman times, when most people lived in small wooden houses.

24

There were ▶
English cathedrals
before 1066, but they
were much smaller
than those built by
the Normans. This
was because the
English were not as
good at building in
stone. You can see
how skilled the
Norman builders
were in this picture.
This is the inside of
Winchester
Cathedral, built on
William the
Conqueror's orders. If
you visit a cathedral,
look out for round
arches like these.
Those will be the bits
built by the Normans.

THE NORMANS IN THE SOUTH

In Norman times, Italy was not a single country. The north was part of the German *Empire*, while the southernmost area was ruled by Greeks. In between, there were several states ruled by the Pope and by a people called the Lombards. The island of Sicily was ruled by Muslim Arabs. These different peoples were often at war with each other and they were always ready to hire foreigners to do their fighting for them. Italy was the perfect place for Norman knights to go to make their fortune.

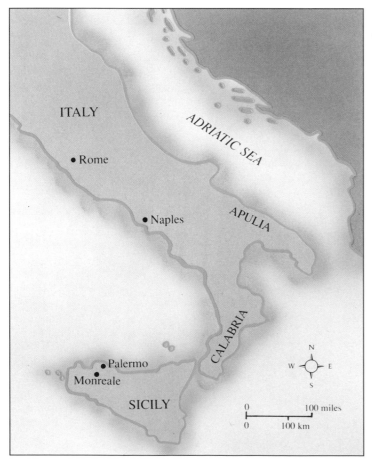

◀ The most successful knights were Robert Guiscard ('The Crafty') and his younger brother Roger. By 1059, the two of them had conquered Apulia and Calabria, which Robert ruled as duke. It was his son Bohemond who went off on the First Crusade (see page 23). Meanwhile, in 1061, Roger had crossed the sea to Sicily and begun a war against the Muslims. By 1071, he was ruling most of the island from his capital, Palermo. In 1130 all the conquests in Italy were joined together into a single kingdom. It was ruled by Roger's son, who called himself King Roger II.

The mosaic shows ▶
King Roger II of
Sicily being crowned
by Christ. Roger was
a successful
conqueror, adding
Malta and part of
Africa to his
kingdom. Unlike most
Norman rulers, he
was also well
educated and could
speak Latin, Greek
and Arabic as well as
French. In this mosaic
Roger is dressed just
like Greek emperors
of the time. He looks
very different from
the short-haired
Normans of the
Bayeux Tapestry. In
fact Roger, who was
born in Italy, probably
didn't even think of
himself as a Norman.

▲ In Sicily, the Normans ruled over a mixed people including many Muslims and Greeks. As a result, the churches of Norman Sicily show a mixture of different styles.

This is part of a Norman monastery at Palermo. It is the cloister, the place where the monks walked. It looks nothing like any cloisters that Normans built in northern Europe. The delicate columns, the rich patterns and the fountain in the foreground were all features of Muslim palaces.

◄ It is only when you look closely at the columns of the monastery at Palermo that you find a clue that this was the work of Normans. Look at the two figures who stand guard on top of this column. They are Norman knights.

GLOSSARY

Archers People who are skilled at using bows and arrows.

Baron A powerful Norman lord. The word, which is French, originally meant simply a 'strong man'.

Bishop A leading churchman. He is head of a group of churches, called a 'diocese'.

Castle A stronghold built by the ruler or his barons.

Cathedral A great church where a bishop had his 'cathedra', or seat.

Church The organization made up of Christians.

Count French title for one of the leading barons. In England they were called earls.

Crusade A Christian holy war, usually against the Muslims who ruled much of the Middle East.

Domesday Book A great survey of England carried out by William the Conqueror. Domesday means 'Judgement Day', the day when Christ was believed to judge everyone in the world. Legal decisions based on the Domesday Book were said to be just as final as Christ's judgement.

Empire A large area of land, including different peoples, ruled by a single state. In Norman times, there were two empires in Europe – the German, or Holy Roman Empire, and the Greek, or Byzantine Empire.

Fallow Land that is left unplanted for a year to regain its goodness.

Middle East A European name for the lands stretching from Egypt to Iran.

Monastery A place where some men went to live and serve God. Women went to live in nunneries.

Monk A man who goes to live in a monastery. Monks promised never to marry, to obey the rules of their order (group of monks) and to live a life of poverty.

Muslim A follower of Islam, the religion started by Muhammad in the seventh century. Muslims believe that there is one God and that Muhammad is the messenger of God.

Nun A woman who promises to serve God and not to marry.

Vikings A name given to the people of Denmark, Norway and Sweden in the ninth and tenth centuries.

IMPORTANT DATES

790s Vikings begin to raid Western Europe.
911 Rolf, a Viking raider, settles in northern France. He becomes first duke of the 'Normans'.
1017 Norman knights begin to travel to southern Italy, hiring themselves out as warriors.
1059 Robert Guiscard ('the Crafty') becomes Duke of Apulia and Calabria.
1061 Robert's younger brother, Roger de Hauteville, begins conquest of Sicily.
1066 Duke William of Normandy conquers England and becomes king.
1081-3 Robert Guiscard invades Greece but is defeated.

1087 William orders a great survey of England, later called the Domesday Book.
1097-1104 The First Crusade. Two of the crusading armies are Norman, led by Robert Curthose, son of William, and Bohemond, son of Robert Guiscard. Bohemond conquers Antioch.
1130 Roger II becomes king of Sicily and southern Italy.
1146-48 Norman fleet from Sicily conquers part of the north African coastline.

BOOKS TO READ

The Children's Book of Domesday England by Peter Bloyden (Kingfisher/English Tourist Board, 1985). You can discover what England was like during William the Conqueror's reign in this book.

Norman Invaders and Settlers by Tony Triggs (Wayland, 1992). This book gives an account of the Norman Conquest and shows you how the Normans lived.

Norman Britain by Tony Triggs (Wayland, 1990). This book uses clues discovered by archaeologists to build up a picture of Norman life.

INDEX